Foxes for Kids

by Judy Schuler
illustrated by John F. McGee

NORTHWORD PRESS
Minnetonka, Minnesota

WILDLIFE *for Kids* **SERIES** ™

DEDICATION
To Kyle

© Judy Schuler, 1998

Photography © 1998: Tom Vezo: front cover; Tom & Pat Leeson: 3, 7, 8-9, 10, 31, 32, 42-43;
D. Robert Franz / The Wildlife Collection: 12-13, 46-47; Bill Silliker, Jr.: 15; David A. Brunetti: 16;
Henry H. Holdsworth / Uniphoto: 19; Nora & Rick Bowers: 22; Bill Lea: 25;
Alan & Sandy Carey: 26-27, 35, 36, 39; Richard Day / Daybreak Imagery: 40, back cover.

NorthWord Press
5900 Green Oak Drive
Minnetonka, MN 55343
1-800-328-3895

Illustrations by John F. McGee / Book design by Russell S. Kuepper

National Wildlife Federation® is the nation's largest conservation, education and advocacy organization.
Since 1936, NWF has educated people from all walks of life to protect nature, wildlife and the world we all share.

Ranger Rick® is an exciting magazine published monthly by National Wildlife Federation®, about wildlife, nature,
and the environment for kids ages 7 to 12. For more information about how to subscribe to this magazine, write or call:
Ranger Rick Department, National Wildlife Federation, 8925 Leesburg Pike, Vienna, Virginia 22184, 1-800-588-1650.

NWF's World Wide Web Site http://www.nwf.org provides instant computer access to information about
National Wildlife Federation, conservation issues and ideas for getting involved in protecting our world.

Library of Congress Cataloging-in-Publication Data
Schuler, Judy,
    Foxes for kids / by Judy Schuler
        p. cm.—(Wildlife for kids series)
        Summary: Relates information about the life, habits, and natural
history of all five North American species of foxes.
        ISBN 1-55971-637-1 (pbk.)
        1. Foxes--Juvenile literature. [1. Foxes.] I. Title.
II. Series
QL737.C22S36   1998   97-5957
599.775--dc21

Printed in Malaysia

Foxes for Kids

Red fox kit

by Judy Schuler
illustrated by John F. McGee

Last year I saw a wild fox! In a clearing near the edge of the forest, I saw a flash of color against the snow. I raised my binoculars for a better look.

A red fox was snuffling around in a snowbank. As I watched, it leaped high in the air and then pounced, sending up a swirling cloud of white powder. It tossed something in the air, and then pounced again. Finally, it lay down to eat. Whatever the fox had caught wasn't very big. In seconds it finished munching and trotted off into the woods.

My name is Maria. In school I learned that although foxes are classified as meat-eaters, or carnivores (CAR-nuh-vorz), they are really omnivores (OM-nuh-vorz). That is, they will eat whatever is handy, plants or animals. They eat fruits such as wild berries, apples, and plums and they will also eat vegetables, mainly corn.

Foxes sometimes raid chicken coops, eating eggs and chickens. Some farmers don't like foxes, but many farmers don't mind them because they keep mice and other rodents out of their grain.

Males are called "dog" foxes. They have scent glands near their tail, near their jaw, and between their toes. They rub the scent on things like trees and rocks to mark their territory and tell other foxes where they live.

Foxes have keen vision.

Pages 8-9: Red fox hunting for food.

The home territory of a fox is about 3 square miles. Foxes usually respect each other's territory, although a young dog fox will sometimes challenge an older male to claim the area as his own.

Red fox dog

The most common fox is the red fox. It can be found almost every-where in North America and Europe. Most red foxes are a rusty orange color. But some can be pale yellow-red to silver-black.

The silver-colored foxes have a mostly black undercoat with longer, silver-tipped outer hairs that are called guard hairs. A cross fox is red with a strip of dark fur down its back and another across its shoulders.

Prey is often hidden from red foxes.

12

Sometimes, more than one color of red fox may be found in the same litter. The one thing all red foxes have in common is the white tip at the end of their tails.

I told my friend, Scott, about seeing the fox, and we decided to look for its den together. A fox den is usually a burrow in the ground. Sometimes they use old dens of other animals like woodchucks.

A female fox is called a vixen. She will often clean out several dens before deciding where she will raise her babies, called kits, pups, or cubs.

Because red foxes build their dens near water, we began searching near a stream that runs through the woods.

Red fox kits resting.

As we walked through the forest, Scott told me a story about a fox that played dead to trick a crow. When the crow came near, hoping for a meal of dead fox, the clever fox sprang to its feet and ate the crow.

Foxes have also been known to trick ducks. After playing with a stick for a while beside a duck pond, a fox will drop the stick and disappear into the forest. Any duck curious about the dropped stick may become the fox's dinner.

Suddenly, Scott stopped and pointed to a hole among some rocks beside the stream.

We were sure it was a den when I saw paw prints in some mud near the hole. But, if the foxes were there, they were hiding deep inside the den. We decided to come back later in the spring.

A well-hidden den.

There are 22 different species of foxes around the world, and 5 of them live in North America. Besides the red fox, there are arctic, kit, swift, and gray foxes. Red foxes are the only ones I have ever seen.

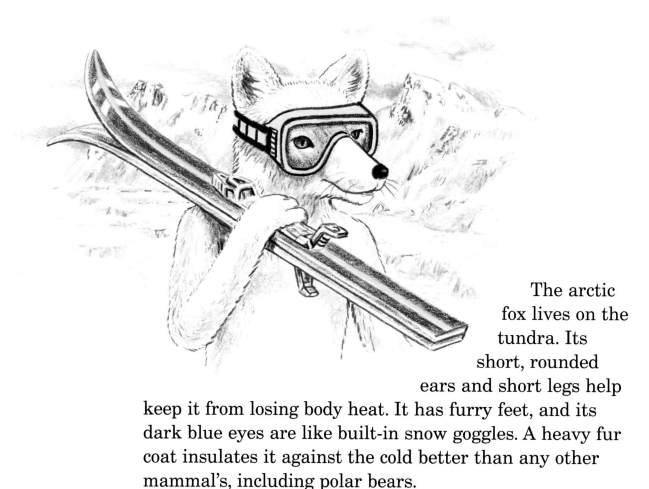

The arctic fox lives on the tundra. Its short, rounded ears and short legs help keep it from losing body heat. It has furry feet, and its dark blue eyes are like built-in snow goggles. A heavy fur coat insulates it against the cold better than any other mammal's, including polar bears.

Arctic foxes need less food to survive than do other animals. This is because of their small size and low metabolism (muh-TAB-o-lizm), which means their body temperature is lower and their heartbeat is slower. Red foxes sleep a lot in the winter to conserve energy. But arctic foxes don't need to. They are active even in very cold weather.

Arctic foxes are usually white in the winter and brown in the summer. But some of them are bluish-gray or brownish-gray. They are darker in summer and lighter in winter. Their fluffy tails are all the same color as their bodies.

Arctic fox

Kit foxes live in the southwestern desert areas of the United States and northern Mexico. Their eyes and furry feet are similar to arctic foxes, but these features protect them from the hot sand and sun of the desert instead of the cold. They have large ears that help get rid of body heat. Their thick fur insulates them from the heat of day as well as the chill of the night. They have a black tip on the end of their long tails.

A diet of mice, voles, birds, and cactus fruits supplies all the moisture kit foxes need. They never have to look for water. I can't imagine never having to take a drink!

The swift fox is quick. It can run up to 40 miles per hour. That's faster than a roadrunner, whose top speed is about 12 miles per hour.

Unlike other foxes, the swift fox uses its dens year-round. It may have as many as 24 different dens. Some are used as shelters from enemies. Some make good cover for raising kits. And some give better protection from the weather.

Swift foxes live from the Texas panhandle north to southern Canada. They also have a black tip at the end of their tails.

Swift fox

Another kind of fox, the gray fox, is the only one that climbs trees. When chased, gray foxes hide in a hole or look for a tree to climb. Sometimes they make their dens in hollow trees. They even jump from branch to branch to look for fruit. One gray fox was seen resting in an empty hawk's nest!

Gray foxes have a black stripe on the top of their tails, and the tip is black. They live from South America through the southern United States, north to the Great Lakes.

Gray fox

In April, Scott and I returned to the den we had found in February. One late afternoon we saw some foxes playing in the grass outside the den.

We found a place behind some brush where we could watch them through our binoculars without bothering them.

Red fox kit

Foxes' sense of smell allows them to find food such as rodents that burrow underground. It also helps them detect enemies even before they see them. They can easily sniff out the border markings of other foxes.

Their keen hearing can pick up the rustling of a mouse in the leaves. I hoped they wouldn't hear us and run away.

Their eyesight is also excellent. Like the eyes of cats, their pupils close into vertical slits. Because of a part of their eyes that reflects light like a mirror, they see very well in the dark.

Foxes are nocturnal (nok-TER-nul), which means they are active at night. They almost always hunt at night, too. During the winter, they sometimes hunt in the daytime if prey is scarce and they are hungry.

In late winter or early spring, 4 to 6 kits are born in the den. If food is scarce and foxes are plentiful, a vixen might only have 2 kits. If there is plenty of food and not very many foxes in an area, she might have a litter as large as 12 kits.

The kits are born blind and toothless. The mother curls around her dark, furry kits to keep them warm. And she covers them with her fluffy tail.

When the kits are 2 weeks old, they open their blue eyes for the first time. By the time they are 4 months old, their eye color has changed to amber and their coats are reddish.

Red fox twin kits

The dog fox brings food to the vixen until the kits are old enough that she can leave them for a while. When the kits are about 4 weeks old, both parents regurgitate (re-GUR-juh-tate), or throw up, food for the kits to eat.

Slowly the kits begin to eat the prey their parents bring back to them. That's how they learn what they will hunt for when they grow up.

The kits we were watching were just starting to hunt, beginning with chasing insects and finding worms. From their parents, they would learn to hunt for small animals such as mice and voles.

By the time they are 6 months old, foxes are pretty much on their own. They are full grown at 9 months and can weigh up to 15 pounds.

Fox kits are prey for large birds such as eagles and hawks, as well as wildcats, bears and coyotes. The parents teach the kits ways to stay safe from predators. They may use their coloring as camouflage to hide, or they use their great speed to outrun enemies.

We noticed that four adult foxes were watching over the kits. Other female foxes sometimes share a den with the mother. They help raise the kits. The father usually helps raise the kits, too.

Red fox kit learning to hunt.

Suddenly, one of the kits wandered away from the others. A vixen quickly ran to it and grabbed it by the back of its neck with her mouth. The kit didn't squirm or wiggle as she carried it back to the others. It just enjoyed the free ride!

Even though foxes are related to dogs, they are also like cats in some ways. They have soft toe pads and hair between their toes. That helps muffle the sound of their footsteps. They also have sensitive whiskers on their noses and paws.

The next day, I went to watch the foxes again. I noticed that they made a lot of different noises. Some of them whined like dogs, and some of them made low, throaty sounds.

I wanted to get closer to see them better, but suddenly they saw me. One of the adults gave a shrill bark, and all of the foxes disappeared into the den.

As the kits grew, the adults began leaving food farther and farther from the den. That encouraged the kits to forage (FOR-ij), or look for food, on their own. The adult foxes would sometimes pounce on a mouse and then drop it in front of a kit, allowing the kit to try to catch the mouse by itself.

Red fox kits learn to hide.

When they play, foxes often crouch low on their front paws, with their rears in the air and their tails wagging. The kits' play-fighting helps them develop self-defense skills that they will need when they are grown.

One day I saw a vixen catch a mouse. Then she dug a hole, not scattering dirt all over the place the way a dog does, but piling it neatly beside the hole. She dropped the mouse into the hole and carefully covered it with the piled dirt. When she had finished hiding it, she brushed the dirt with her whiskers.

Another fox might be able to find the mouse by its smell, but it didn't look like anything was buried there. Foxes hide their food when they have had plenty to eat. It's called caching (KASH-ing). This way they have something to eat later when food might be scarce.

Foxes usually live 5 or 6 years in the wild. Healthy adult foxes aren't easy prey, but sometimes they are caught off-guard by a predator.

Scott and I continued watching the foxes for the rest of the summer, but by August the den was often empty. The family was breaking up.

Red fox kits exploring.

Soon, the young males would begin looking for their own territories. Some females might stay to help raise their mother's next litter. Others would look for new den sites in which to raise their own kits.

By the time school started in the fall, we seldom saw a fox near the den. I am going to miss watching the foxes during the winter, but I know I will see them outside again, probably by late January.

I can't wait to watch the new family learn and grow and play!

Pages 46-47: This red fox den is full.

Other titles available in our popular

WILDLIFE ⟨For Kids⟩ SERIES

Bats *For Kids*
Order # 1139 • ISBN # 1-55971-545-6

Bears *For Kids*
Order # 1009 • ISBN # 1-55971-134-5

Beavers *For Kids*
Order # 1153 • ISBN # 1-55971-576-6

Bison *For Kids*
Order # 1084 • ISBN # 1-55971-431-X

Butterflies *For Kids*
Order # 1144 • ISBN # 1-55971-546-4

Dolphins *For Kids*
Order # 1099 • ISBN # 1-55971-460-3

Eagles *For Kids*
Order # 1008 • ISBN # 1-55971-133-7

Hawks *For Kids*
Order # 1079 • ISBN # 1-55971-462-X

Kangaroos *For Kids*
Order # 1071 • ISBN # 1-55971-595-2

Loon Magic *For Kids*
Order # 1002 • ISBN # 1-55971-121-3

Manatees *For Kids*
Order # 1106 • ISBN # 1-55971-539-1

Moose *For Kids*
Order # 1056 • ISBN # 1-55971-211-2

Owls *For Kids*
Order # 1117 • ISBN # 1-55971-475-1

Pandas *For Kids*
Order # 1097 • ISBN # 1-55971-594-4

Raccoons *For Kids*
Order # 1063 • ISBN # 1-55971-229-5

Sharks *For Kids*
Order # 1101 • ISBN # 1-55971-476-X

Whales *For Kids*
Order # 1005 • ISBN # 1-55971-125-6

Whitetails *For Kids*
Order # 1003 • ISBN # 1-55971-122-1

Wild Horses *For Kids*
Order # 1082 • ISBN # 1-55971-465-4

Wolves *For Kids*
Order # 1004 • ISBN # 1-55971- 123-X

See your nearest book seller
or order by phone 1-800-328-3895

NORTHWORD
NORTHWORD PRESS